CASTLES

Susan Churchill

Illustrated by Brett Breckon & Trevor Parkin

Contents

A DESIGN EYE BOOK

This edition published by Barnes & Noble, Inc.,
by arrangement with Design Eye Publishing
1998 Barnes & Noble Books

ISBN 0-7607-0891-6

1 3 5 7 9 10 8 6 4 2

Designed by Olwen Fowler

Manufactured in China

Introduction

Welcome to the spectacular, brutal and exciting world of medieval castles! Home to wealthy lords and barons, castles were built at a time when Europe was just a collection of territories and small states. Kings, princes and barons were all competing for power and needed strong fortresses to defend themselves against their enemies.

With this Ultimate Explorer kit, you will be able to discover every aspect of castle life, from feasting to tournaments to bloody battles. Meet the baron who owned the castle and all the other characters who lived and worked there. Find out what life was like in the castle, how people enjoyed themselves in peace time and how they fought off violent attacks.

Many barons had several castles and a great deal of land. They would travel from castle to castle so they could make sure everything was being run properly. The baron and his household had to be fed from food grown by the ordinary people living around each castle, so they were not always welcome visitors!

Everyone knew their place in medieval society. The baron was one of the most wealthy noblemen. His lands were given to him by the king in return for his loyalty and a promise to supply an army in time of war. Below him were the knights or lesser lords, and then the peasants – the poorest people who worked the land.

Your Ultimate Explorer is much more than just a book. The kit also includes a historically accurate pop-down castle, models to make and activities to carry out. You will find a model catapult, soldiers to paint and even a royal scroll for you to fill in.

As you read the book, you'll find special castle boxes directing you to items of particular interest in the pop-down castle. If you can't find something, have a look at the colour castle poster!

Separate activity scrolls refer you to exciting projects. You'll find detailed instructions for these on the black and white activity poster.

Now read on to discover the brutal and ruthless world of medieval castles for yourself…

Building a Castle

The walls might be as much as 4 metres (13 feet) thick and were usually built in three layers. There was rough stone on the inside, fitted 'ashlar' blocks on the outside and a flint and rubble filling in the middle. Everything was held together with mortar made from sand, water and lime.

Building a castle was costly and labour-intensive, and could take many years. An army of workers was needed to cut and manhandle stone for the walls, and with only primitive wheelbarrows, pulleys and windlasses to help them, the builders relied on sheer muscle power. Stone castles first became common in the mid-12th century. At this period, they often consisted of a stone tower or 'keep', perhaps protected by an inner wall. Lower outer walls with round 'mural' towers might be added later to give a second line of defence. Your pop-down castle shows all of these.

Castle building was never complete. This picture shows a new gatehouse being constructed in the 14th century to strengthen the defences of a much older castle.

Castle Builders

All new building projects were put in the hands of a master mason, who planned the building and supervised the work. He and his assistants ordered the building materials and hired the workforce. The masons shaped the blocks of fine stone ('ashlar') and carved decorative stonework for windows and doors. Meanwhile, carpenters sawed planks for scaffolding, floors and roof timbers. Other jobs were done by roughmasons, who built the walls, blacksmiths, who made tools and fittings, labourers who mixed the mortar and dug ditches, and a well-digger.

Skilled stonemasons were highly respected and well-paid. They organised their work from the covered 'lodge' or work hut on the building site. Each lodge had strict rules about working practices, and supervised the young apprentices who learned their craft on site.

Activities

Before a baron could build a castle, he had to receive permission from the king.

Your Ultimate Explorer has a royal scroll giving YOU a licence to build a castle. Read the instructions in the activity poster to find out how to fill it in.

You can also make your own royal crown – the ultimate symbol of power. Again there are instructions in the activity poster, and your kit contains sparkling jewels for added decoration.

Tour of the Castle

Inside the walls of many castles stood an impressive great tower or 'keep'. This was the home of the baron and his family and the heart of castle life. The entrance was often on the first floor, out of reach of the battering ram. Inside, there may have been kitchens and a 'garrison', or guard room, stacked with weapons for the castle's defence. Above, on the second floor, you might have found the great hall and a chapel. The baron's private rooms – a bedroom and an outer chamber – were usually at the top of the tower. On the ground floor, there may have been storerooms for food and drink, a well, and grim dungeons.

The keep or great tower was the most important part of the castle. Keeps often had a single spiral stone staircase connecting the different floors. It always wound upwards in a clockwise direction to make it difficult for attacking knights to wield their swords.

Outside the Keep

Numerous other buildings were added to provide for the needs of the baron and to enable the castle to be self-sufficient. There might have been a granary to keep grain for making flour, a brewhouse to make the castle's beer, forges for the blacksmith and armourer, and a wood store.

The stables had to be large to accommodate the horses of the baron, his knights and visiting guests. There would have been heavy work horses for pulling wagons, strong war horses and smaller, faster horses for hunting.

In the Castle

Castles didn't have flushing toilets. Instead you went to a 'garderobe' – a primitive toilet that was simply a hole over a long chute! Can you find the garderobes in your pop-down castle? What about the unfortunate 'gong farmer' who had to clean them out?

Within the outer wall there may have been stables, kennels for hunting dogs and 'mews' for falcons. There may also have been a fishpond, and gardens for herbs, vegetables and fruit trees.

From Dawn to Dusk

The castle day started early. Just before dawn the first servants rolled up their straw-filled mattresses or 'pallets' from the floors of the kitchen and the great hall, and lit the fires. Everyone else rose at dawn. The baron and his lady would dress and then go to a service in the chapel. Afterwards they joined everybody in the great hall for a breakfast of bread and ale. Even the children drank ale – it was safer than water, which often made people ill. Once breakfast was over, the baron and his lady gave their instructions to the servants and the castle became a hive of activity.

The Day goes by

When she was not supervising the running of the household, the lady of the castle spent her time with other noble ladies – friends and relations – doing embroidery, weaving, or maybe listening to travelling performers called troubadours singing popular songs and ballads.

The baron's family and the castle servants might gather in the main hall again at 10 or 11 in the morning for the main meal of the day. Then work continued until supper, at about 5 o'clock, when plenty of ale and wine were consumed. At the end of the meal, the tables would be cleared away and there might be entertainment: a travelling jester or acrobat might perform and minstrels would sing and play music in the gallery. The ladies often went to their rooms early, leaving the men to their revelry. When the baron left for his comfortable curtained bed, the servants would unroll their pallets again and put out the candles for the night.

The baron's sons had lessons with the castle priest, writing with pointed sticks on wax tablets. As well as basic subjects like reading and writing, they were taught Latin and French. Education wasn't considered necessary for girls, who learned how to run a household from their mothers or a noble lady in another castle.

In the Castle

Children performed many jobs around the castle. Can you find a child looking after hens in the garden?

The armourer was constantly in demand, making repairs to armour and weapons and ensuring that the castle had ample supplies of arrows, crossbow bolts and other weapons.

The Baron's Household

The baron needed a whole range of officials and servants to ensure that life in the castle ran smoothly, and that he kept control of his land. The two most important officials were normally noblemen and friends of the baron: the chamberlain (or treasurer), who kept the baron's accounts, and the steward, who looked after his farmland, woodland and tenants.

The steward was helped by the bailiff, who organised the farmwork from day to day, allotting jobs to the peasants and keeping everything in good repair. In turn, he was helped by the reeve, who was elected by the peasants and oversaw their work.

The baron met his steward regularly to keep up-to-date with the management of his land. He made all the important decisions and his officials saw that they were carried out.

Next in importance after the steward and chamberlain were the constable and the marshal. The constable was responsible for the castle's defence and the garrison – the men who defended the castle; the marshal organised horses and outdoor servants like the carters and huntsmen.

Castle Servants

The baron's wife was in charge of household matters and had her own steward, who was responsible for buying food and drink and supervising kitchen and serving staff. These included the 'pantler', who looked after the food supplies; the butler (a nobleman) who organised the castle's wine supplies in the 'buttery'; the 'ewerer', who ensured the baron's tablecloths and napkins were clean; and the chief cook, under-cooks, and 'scullions' who did the menial jobs. There were also laundresses, matweavers, a falconer, grooms, blacksmiths and armourers, sweepers to clear away horse dung and 'gong farmers' to clean out the garderobe pits.

Activity

Moulded into the lid of your Ultimate Explorer kit is a picture of a noble baron.

Following the instructions on your activity poster, why not make a 'brass' rubbing of this design?

Ewerer Chief Cook Maid Falconer Blacksmith Laundress Armourer Gong Farmer

Cooks and Scullions

All the worst jobs in the kitchen were done by young boys called 'scullions'. They cleaned the cooking pots, washed the dishes, turned the spit in front of the blazing hot fire and fetched the water from the well.

When the baron was in residence, the castle kitchens were always busy. As well as the baron, his family and guests, there were the guards and the servants to feed. All the food preparation and cooking was supervised by the head cook who would bellow orders over the noise of chopping and pounding.

Most of the food was cooked over the open fire in the fireplace. Meat, vegetables and puddings were boiled in an iron pot over the fire, and whole carcasses of meat could be roasted on a spit. The kitchen was a hot place to work and there was a constant risk of fire.

A Rich Diet

A castle was kept well-stocked with food to cater for the baron and any unexpected guests. A good food supply was absolutely essential if the castle was in danger of being besieged – the lives of everyone depended on it.

The range of food available to rich people was impressive. They were partial to meat, and ate beef, pork, mutton, deer and wild boar. They also ate birds as diverse as peacocks, swans, blackbirds and greenfinches. Milk from cows, sheep and goats was used in puddings and to make cream, butter and cheese, which were known as 'white meats'.

In the Castle

Can you find the castle oven? You should be able to see a cook taking out a loaf of bread.

Although the storerooms were cool, food didn't keep for long. Unless eaten immediately after being killed, meat was smoked or salted in wooden vats to preserve it. A lot of meat was salted at the beginning of winter, because there wasn't enough fodder to keep all the animals alive. Vegetables and fruit were dried or pickled.

Activity

Why not try baking some delicious 'medieval' cakes? You'll find full instructions on your activity poster.

Bread was made from flour ground in the baron's mill and baked in the castle kitchens. Finely milled flour was used to make white bread for the baron and nobles; the servants ate coarse brown bread.

The Medieval Knight

The knights were the military elite, and commanded respect as they went about their business at the castle. They were all noblemen who had sworn their loyalty to the king and the baron. Most would have their own estates, given to them by the baron. In return they would have to spend a specified number of months every year helping to guard the castle.

At a medium sized castle, there would have been about twelve knights, who came and went on a rota system. They acted as the baron's companions and bodyguards, joining him when he inspected his lands or went hunting and hawking.

Only the wealthy could afford to become knights. As a mounted warrior, a knight was expected to pay for his own warhorses, armour and weaponry, as well as the services of a squire and armed followers. The sword and lance were his main weapons, but he also carried a dagger and sometimes a short-handled axe.

In the Castle

Can you find the baron's armour in his bedchamber?

Heraldry

When he rode into battle, a knight needed to show his identity. He did this by decorating his 'surcoat' (the tunic that covered his armour) and shield with a design that belonged to him alone.

The surcoat became known as a 'coat of arms', which is what we now call the designs themselves. Coats of arms were used on armour, flags, seals and above the gatehouses of castles. Each one passed to the eldest son when his father died.

Although fighting men, knights were expected to behave honourably on and off the battlefield. Their so-called 'chivalric' code of behaviour also involved defending the church, protecting the weak and honouring and serving noble ladies.

Activity

Add a coat of arms to your castle scroll.

Coats of arms were designed by heralds, who kept a record of them in books called armorials. It was also a herald's job to introduce participating knights at tournaments, and to list those knights killed in battle by identifying their coats of arms as they lay on the battlefield.

Pages and Squires

By serving their lord and other knights, pages and squires learned that the highest honour was to serve others. At meals, young pages brought dishes to the table; squires carved the meat and poured the wine.

The castle courtyard often rang with screeches and shouts as young boys wrestled and practised fighting with wooden staves, blunt wooden swords and shields. These were some of the 'pages' and 'squires' who were sent to the castle to train to be knights. The sons of neighbouring noblemen, they were all entrusted to the baron at seven years old to serve as pages. They were taught polite manners by serving at table and attending on noble ladies, and learned how to ride and handle falcons. At fourteen a page became a squire and was apprenticed to a knight. A squire looked after his knight's armour and horses and perfected the fighting skills he would need to follow his master into battle.

A squire normally became a knight at 21. After a night of prayer in the chapel and a ceremonial bath, he was dressed and given his sword and spurs. He was made a knight with a tap of a sword on each shoulder, usually by the knight who trained him, or by the king.

Training to Fight

Pages and squires learned fighting skills from an early age. From wooden swords, they progressed to heavier weapons, sometimes training with weapons twice the weight of those used in battle to build up their muscles. They learned to shoot with crossbows and longbows and became skilled horsemen, practising riding with one hand to keep their sword arm free. They also had to get used to fighting in armour and practised 'tilting' (jousting) at the quintain, a wooden pole with a swinging shield and weighted bag at the top, to train for the tournament.

In the Castle

Squires would clean their knight's armour by rolling it in a barrel of sand and vinegar. Can you find a squire doing this?

Tilting at the quintain helped a squire to develop quick reactions. He had to hold or 'couch' the lance correctly to hit the target, then he had to make a quick getaway to avoid being hit by the heavy weight that swung round afterwards!

The Fighting Force

High up on the castle walls, archers and crossbowmen would keep watch, patrolling the 'wallwalk' behind the battlements. Others guarded the gatehouse and checked visitors and members of the baron's household in and out. These were all members of the 'garrison', the castle's fighting force. Some were knights, who supervised their own groups of men-at-arms and bowmen. Others were men hired by the baron with money paid by knights who chose not to do their castle duty.

All the members of the garrison were responsible to the constable, who looked after the castle's defences and lived in the gatehouse, where he could keep an eye on things.

Archers needed strong arms to pull a longbow and practised constantly to maintain their strength and skill. There were practice targets called butts for the garrison to use inside the castle walls, and others outside the church in the village so peasants could practise after Mass on Sundays.

In the Castle

How many crossbowmen can you find patrolling the castle walls?

Lethal Weapons

The longbow was given its name because it was longer than earlier bows. As tall as the archer himself, it could fire arrows a distance of about 300 metres, which made it a particularly useful weapon in open battle. Longbows were made from yew, elm or birch wood. The arrows had a shaft of ash, goose-feather 'fletchings' and an iron arrowhead. There were different arrowheads for different targets: a small, flat one for general use; a wide, barbed head for animals; and a needle-like one for piercing armour.

Crossbows were used as early as Roman times and were powerful, deadly weapons. They fired short arrows called bolts with iron tips that could pierce full armour at 50 metres. Their only drawback was that they were slow to reload – a longbowman could fire up to 12 arrows for every bolt from a crossbow.

Reloading a crossbow wasn't a problem when it was used in castle defence – the crossbowman could take cover behind the battlements while he prepared his weapon to fire the next bolt. To speed things up, he might work with an assistant who loaded one crossbow while he was firing another.

Under Threat

If the castle came under attack, the defenders would try to fight off the attackers with all the weapons they had to hand. They might set up catapults on the battlements to fire at the attacking force, while archers and crossbowmen would be positioned along the outer walls.

If the baron discovered that an enemy force was heading for the castle, there might be only a few days to lay in provisions and strengthen the defences. The baron would order the building of wooden hoardings around the battlements; weak masonry would be repaired; trees near the castle would be cut down to deny the attackers cover and wood for siege weapons, while messengers would be sent out to bring reinforcements. Meanwhile, the armourer would start making extra supplies of arrows and bolts, which members of the garrison would take to strategic positions throughout the castle.

The defenders built special hoardings or 'brattices' – battlements that jutted out from the wall with holes in the floor so defenders could drop scalding water, hot sand or rocks on attackers below. Cold water could also be poured through the holes to put out fires at the base of the wall.

Under cover of darkness, the defenders might make a surprise attack on the enemy camp. Using a hidden door in the castle walls called a 'sally port' or 'postern gate' they might try to destroy enemy siege engines, or set fire to tents and food supplies.

Sometimes local villagers were allowed into their lord's castle for protection, although they would share the castle's fate. They might bring their valuable livestock with them as a source of food.

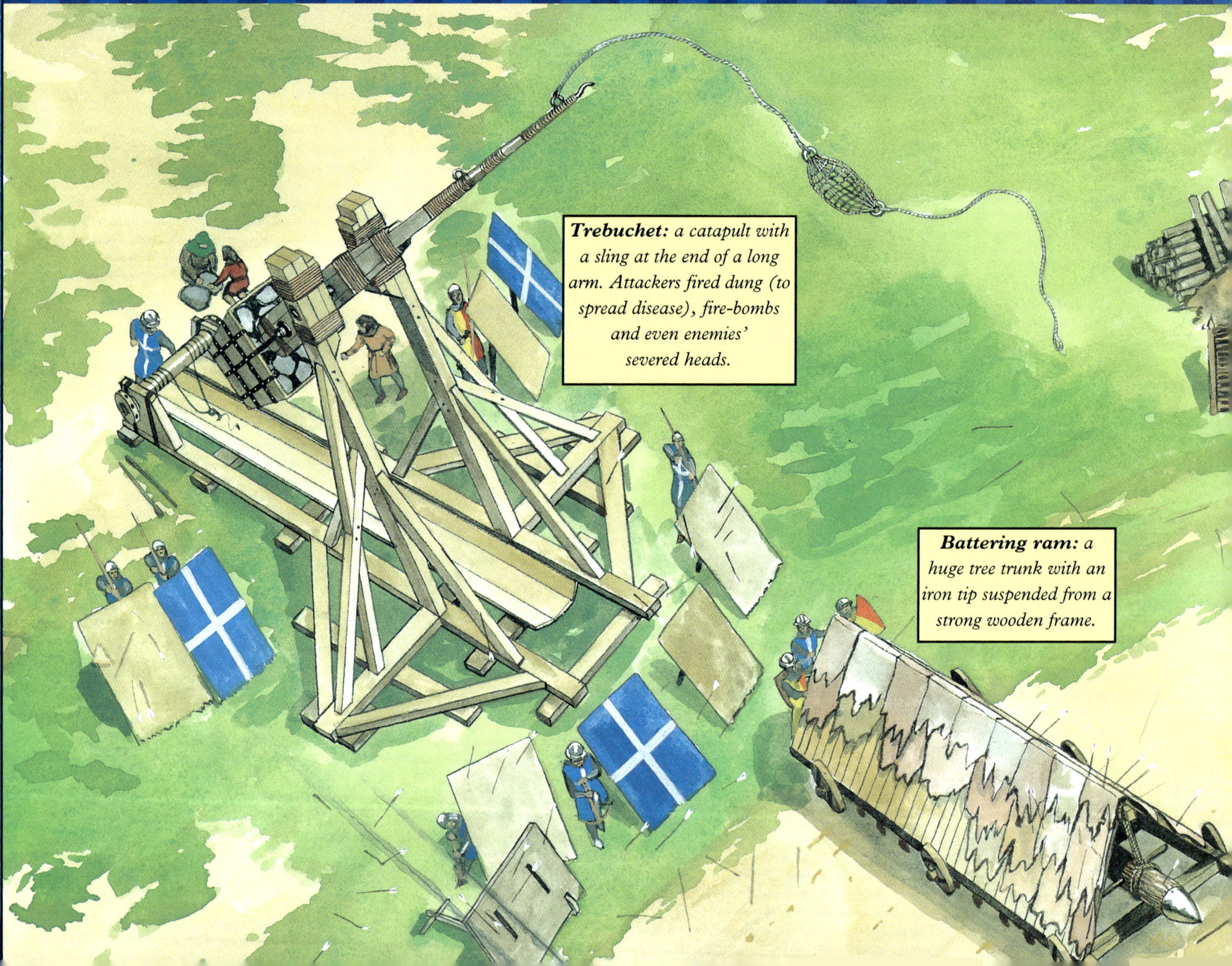

Trebuchet: *a catapult with a sling at the end of a long arm. Attackers fired dung (to spread disease), fire-bombs and even enemies' severed heads.*

Battering ram: *a huge tree trunk with an iron tip suspended from a strong wooden frame.*

UNDER ATTACK

The attack is on! A full-scale attack was brutal and violent, and cost many lives. Both sides used simple but highly effective war machines to bombard the enemy with missiles, while archers unleashed a rain of arrows...

The Attackers Arrive

As soon as they arrived, the enemy force would often make a demand for the castle to surrender. If the defenders accepted, they were allowed to leave the castle unharmed.

If they refused, the attackers might decide to starve them into submission by cutting off their food supplies. Eventually, the defenders would be forced to eat rats, dogs, and even grass, tree bark and leather to survive.

Preparing a full scale Attack

A siege could go on for months, and conditions for the attackers could be grim. It was often difficult to ensure adequate food supplies for a long period, and in the summer many died of a disease called dysentry.

If winter was on its way, a long siege would be almost impossible. Life in the besiegers' camp would become more and more miserable as biting winds and snow replaced long summer days. The commander of the attacking force would have only one option: a full-scale assault.

In the attackers' camp, there would be plenty to be done. Massive siege weapons had to be assembled from parts brought in by wagon. Among them were the mangonel for hurling stones and boulders, the ballista for firing enormous bolts, and the siege tower for archers to fire from. Meanwhile, swords would be sharpened, arrows prepared, and longbows strung. The leader of the attacking force would be busy issuing commands and checking that everything was in place. Then the battle would begin...

Activity

Assemble your model mangonel, then set up a siege scene on the castle with your model soldiers.

Ballista: *a giant crossbow.*
Its huge bolt was so powerful it could go through several people at once.

Wooden shields *protected attacking archers and crossbowmen from enemy fire.*

Mining: *a tunnel was dug towards the castle wall, shored up by timbers as it progressed. Once under the foundations, the props were destroyed, the roof collapsed and the castle wall came tumbling down.*

Siege tower: *archers inside could pick off defenders, then cross onto the battlements for an assault on the castle.*

Life on the Land

Beyond the walls of many castles lay a small village – often just 20 or 30 thatched huts made from wattle and daub (woven twigs held together with clay, dung and chopped straw) dotted around a stone church. These were the homes of the peasants who farmed the baron's fields. In return they were allowed to cultivate strips of land and small vegetable plots for themselves. Their life was a constant struggle. Every day, except Sundays and 'holy days', they worked from dawn to dusk to produce food for their families, as well as the baron's household. If the crops failed, many would starve to death. There was no other food.

Each family tended its own strips in the large, open fields, where they grew wheat or rye and barley. For the big jobs, like ploughing, they pooled their resources. Everyone helped with the haymaking and the harvest.

The Peasants' Lot

In medieval times, most of the peasants were 'villeins', farmworkers who were literally owned by the lord of the manor. The lord laid down strict rules about the work they had to do for him throughout the year and these rules were enforced by the reeve and bailiff. In addition, peasants had to grind their corn in the lord's mill and bake their bread in his ovens, services they paid for with a proportion of their flour and bread.

Villeins could do almost nothing without the baron's permission. The only way they could gain their freedom was to save money to buy land of their own, marry a free person or flee the village and escape capture for a year and a day.

In summer, the peasants grazed their lambs, cows and goats on the rough common land, keeping a look-out for bears and wolves.

The Hunt

Hunting dogs were highly prized and different breeds were trained to track scent, to chase and to bring down the quarry. Alaunts (wolfhounds) were powerful dogs but needed armoured collars to protect them from a boar's vicious tusks.

The blast of hunting horns was a common sound in the forests surrounding medieval castles. As dogs chased through the undergrowth barking with excitement, the baron and his knights would ride close behind, boar spears at the ready.

Hunting gave the knights a chance to practise their riding and weapon skills, keeping them trained for war. Sometimes they hunted on horseback with swords and crossbows or spears; sometimes they lay in wait with longbows – the only time they used this weapon – while men called beaters worked with the dogs to drive the prey towards them. Hunting also provided valuable meat for the table. Stag was the most sought-after quarry, then wild boar, deer, wolves, bears, foxes and hares. Anyone found 'poaching' (catching birds or animals on the baron's land) was punished severely. Offenders might have their right hand chopped off and were sometimes hanged.

hawking

In the Castle

Find the huntsman entering the kitchen with the animals and birds killed while hunting and hawking.

More refined than hunting, hawking was popular with noblemen and ladies. The type of bird you hunted with depended on your rank in society – an eagle for an emperor, a gyrfalcon for a king or queen, a peregrine falcon for a lord and a hawk for a noblewoman. A favourite falcon might be kept in the lord's chamber, but most were looked after by the castle falconer and kept in a long wooden shed in the castle called a mews. The falconer would accompany the hawking party, who set out on horseback, many carrying their own birds on their gloved fists.

Falcons and hawks were used to catch rabbits, hares and all kinds of birds. Until ready to hunt they were held by leather straps called jesses attached to their legs and their heads were hooded to keep them calm.

Medieval pastimes

Most members of the baron's household were kept too busy to have much leisure time, but when the castle was at peace and the household duties were completed, the noble ladies, knights, squires and pages enjoyed a range of games and activities.

The baron's young children might play with wooden hoops, carts, tops, dolls and skipping ropes. Older pages and squires spent a lot of time learning to ride, wrestle and play ball games like football and a kind of hockey (both played with an animal's bladder). Children and adults alike played board games, while games like blind man's buff, tag and pick-a-back were also very popular.

Peasant children spent most of their time helping at home and in the fields, but on Sundays and summer evenings they made their own entertainment improvising swings and see-saws and playing rough-and-tumble games.

Even in play, children spent a lot of time learning adult skills. Boys learnt to ride and fight but, like the girls, also enjoyed music, dancing and board games.

The castle garden was usually a tranquil spot where fruit, herbs and vegetables were grown for the lord's table. It was the perfect place for a secluded walk, and many knights and ladies met there.

Culture & Refinement

Inside the ladies' room or 'solar', the ladies did spinning, weaving and embroidery. They also played music and sang, and read fashionable stories of love and chivalry.

The baron and his knights were welcome to visit but they were expected to be on their best behaviour. They might stop to play a board game like chess, draughts, chequers or backgammon or to listen to a storyteller reciting poems about legendary heroes.

In the Castle

Can you find two people playing a board game?

Activity

Recreate the flavour of medieval life by playing the King's Challenge game, which is based on an authentic medieval game called Fox and Geese.

All the rules are explained on your activity poster.

Medieval music

In the evening when the meal was over and the trestle tables cleared away, the great hall of the castle would echo to the sound of laughter, dancing – and music.

Music played an important part in medieval life. In palaces and castles, kings and nobles dined to the sound of harps and lutes. In churches and cathedrals, priests and monks chanted psalms and prayers, unaccompanied by musical instruments, in a form of singing known as plainsong. On feast days and festivals the poor would sing folk songs and dance to the lively music of the pipe and drums. Ladies and knights would listen attentively to poems recited to musical accompaniment by entertainers called minstrels and troubadours.

Minstrels often toured from castle to castle, entertaining lords and ladies with music and poetry. At feasts they played instrumental music during the food courses and accompanied other entertainers during the intervals. Their instruments included the harp, the lute and the fiddle.

Minstrels & Troubadours

Medieval minstrels were versatile entertainers. Not only could they play a number of different instruments and improvise music as they performed, they could often also mime, imitate bird and animal sounds, juggle or do acrobatic tricks. Their songs told of the heroic deeds of great warriors of the past, which had a particular appeal for the knights listening to them.

Troubadours specialised in writing and performing poems about love. Unlike minstrels, they were usually educated noblemen who understood chivalry and the art of romance.

Not all minstrels and troubadours were men. There were some very accomplished lady troubadours attached to particular courts who were said to be beautiful, noble and well-educated.

Hand drums were a popular accompaniment to dancing since they gave a strong beat. 'Nakers' were usually hung from a belt in pairs. The tabor was a single drum played with a drumstick or the hand.

In the Castle

Find the minstrel practising in the courtyard.

THE CHURCH & EDUCATION

The chapel was central to castle life. The baron and his family attended Mass every day, while servants and peasants went at least once a week.

The church taught that if people followed the teachings of Christ, they would find eternal happiness when they died; if they sinned, they would burn forever in the flames of hell. Because death was such a constant feature of medieval life for the rich and the poor (who were lucky to live to 30), this was a powerful message. As a result, the church grew rich and influential, with its own taxes, laws and courts.

In medieval times, the Catholic church was all-powerful. Services were conducted in Latin, so ordinary people knew the stories of the bible only through the carvings, wall paintings and stained glass windows that decorated churches and cathedrals.

Reading & Writing

Activities

All important documents had to carry the 'seal' or stamp of their author. You can add a royal seal to your scroll using the wax and king stamp in your kit. Just follow the instructions on the activity poster.

The only people with any real education were the clergy – the castle chaplain, the village priest, and the monks and nuns who lived in abbeys, monasteries and convents. In noble families, the castle chaplain usually taught pages and squires to read and write, and girls were sometimes sent to a convent to be taught by nuns.

The only schools were the 'grammar' schools, attached to cathedrals and large churches, where boys spent nine hours a day learning to read, write and speak Latin fluently before tackling subjects like arithmetic, geometry and astronomy. From here they might go into the church, or go on to study law or medicine.

Plays featuring some of the more momentous bible stories were a popular form of entertainment. Performed at the end of church services, often in church porches, they became known as 'mystery' plays.

Books were rare and highly treasured, because each one was written and illustrated by hand. Some of the most beautiful were produced by monks in monasteries, who painted miniature pictures in brightly coloured paints and often started each page with a decorative gold letter.

Health & Hygiene

There was no anaesthetic to deaden the pain of an operation, so patients were often given wine or ale to drink before the surgeon began. Sometimes they were held down by friends or tied to the operating table.

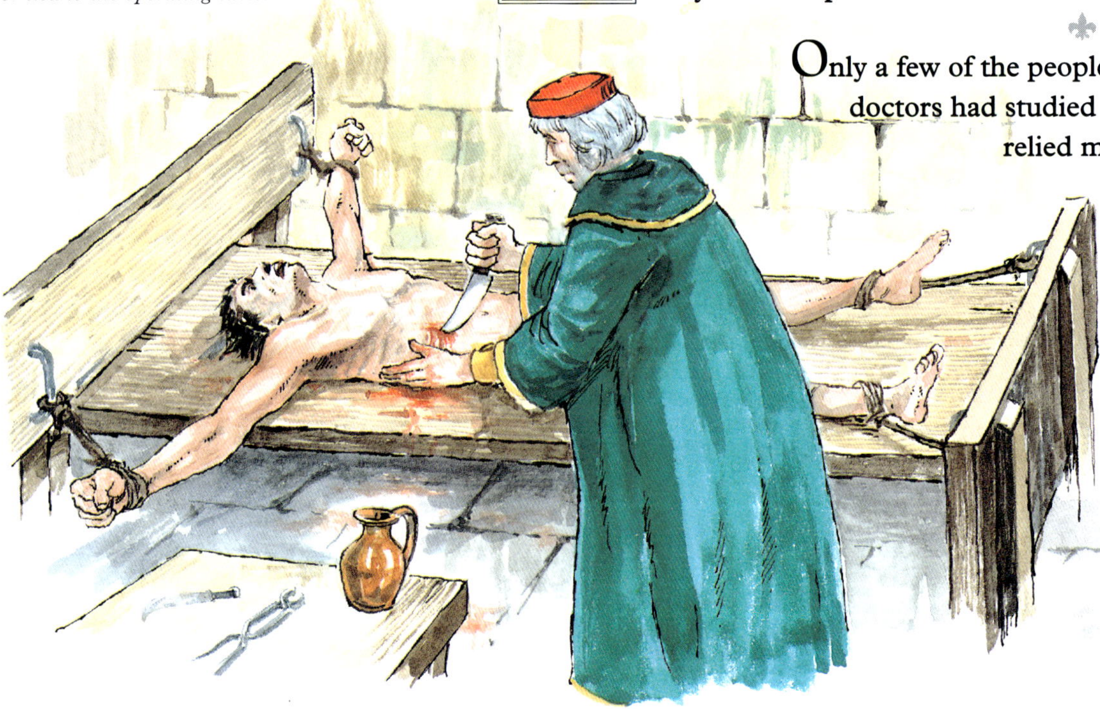

In medieval times, knowledge about disease and the human body was very limited. Herbal medicines were very popular and herbs like Lemon Balm were grown specially in the castle grounds. They often helped to cure minor illnesses.

Only a few of the people who called themselves doctors had studied medicine – and even they relied mostly on superstition and guesswork. Many of those who carried out operations were barbers with little or no medical training. Their success rate was not high, and many routine treatments such as blood letting (where the patient was made to bleed) actually reduced the chances of recovery.

Clean is Best

The best way to live long was to stay fit and healthy, but the importance of hygiene and the link between dirt and disease wasn't understood. Rich people could afford to take fairly regular hot baths in a wooden tub and used soap made from animal fat or olive oil scented with herbs. They also cleaned their teeth with a kind of toothpaste made from ground shells, and sweetened their breath with honey or aromatic herbs and spices. Poor people did not have such luxuries, and in the towns the contents of chamber pots were thrown directly out of the window and into the street, where people wore special raised wooden shoes called pattens to keep their feet out of the muck.

The surgeon's basic instruments were a sharp knife and primitive forceps (often used for extracting arrowheads). They were probably used without being sterilised and as a result many patients died from infected wounds.

In the Castle

Find the herb garden in the castle grounds.

Medicines were made from all kinds of unlikely ingredients. The most effective were probably drinks and poultices (ointments) made from herbs. Many herbal remedies are still used today.

Crime & Punishment

From time to time, the baron and his steward would preside over the local court, normally in the Great Hall of the castle. This is where crimes against the baron and his estate were tried and grievances between villagers were sorted out. A peasant might stand accused of chopping down trees on the baron's land, or of grinding his own corn, or maybe of brawling with his neighbours. If, in the view of the responsible villagers present, he was guilty, the baron would pass sentence. Minor offences were punished by fines, the pillory or whipping. More serious crimes, like murder and theft of more than a shilling were dealt with by touring judges and were punishable by beheading, burning or hanging.

Ordinary criminals were rarely imprisoned. The only prisoners in the castle dungeons were likely to be political prisoners – knights or their followers who were suspected of bertraying the baron or the king.

Prisoners were often manacled to the wall of the dungeon or prison room with a heavy chain. Sometimes they were lowered into a dark hole through a trapdoor; this was known as an 'oubliette' - a place where the prisoner might be left and forgotten.

A day in the pillory was an uncomfortable experience. Not only would your body ache, but all the other villagers would taunt you and throw stones and rotten vegetables.

In the Castle

Can you find the prisoners in the dungeon?

Knights who fell foul of the law or broke their oath of loyalty shared the same harsh punishment as common folk. They might be stripped of their armour and dragged along the ground behind horses, or paraded through the streets before execution.

Anyone caught red-handed stealing property or poaching on the baron's land was likely to be punished on the spot. If the culprit was lucky he might lose his right hand; if not, he would be hanged.

FAIRS & FESTIVALS

The annual fair was one of the high points of the year. Most large towns had markets every week where local peasants could sell spare produce and livestock, and traders and pedlars sold pots, pans, knives, tools, cloth and leather goods. But the fair was a much grander occasion. Usually held just once a year and lasting several weeks at a time, it would draw merchants and traders from all over Europe as well as local tradesmen and farmers.

As well as the stalls, there would be jugglers, acrobats, puppet shows, dancing bears and travelling musicians to entertain the fair-goers. Cook houses sold meat pies and hot meals and there would be plenty of cheap wine and ale to aid the merry-making.

Days of Rest

Many fairs were held on saints' feast days and some grew up around religious festivals, when the town's population was swelled by pilgrims who often travelled hundreds of miles to take part in special church services. Feast days and holy days were an important part of the medieval calendar. There were about 50 each year, besides Sundays. Although not all were holidays, most people were allowed 15 or 20 to celebrate the main religious festivals of Christmas, Easter and Whitsuntide. Other festivities, like May Day, Midsummer Eve and Halloween, dated back to pre-Christian times and celebrated the cycle of the seasons.

May Day revellers celebrated the coming of spring by crowning the 'King and Queen of the May' with garlands and dancing round the Maypole. Green foods were served on green parsley bread trenchers.

Medieval Christmas celebrations lasted for twelve days. The rich and the poor decorated their homes with holly, ivy and mistletoe, and burned a special 'Yule' log in the hearth. Peasants were usually invited to a grand Christmas feast in the castle, where there would be games, music and dancing.

TOURNAMENTS

Tournaments were spectacular events. The most popular form of knightly combat, they allowed the participants to display their courage and skill in a one-to-one encounter – and they also gave them the chance to practise for battle. A fight would begin with a fanfare of trumpets as the mounted knights took their places at opposite ends of a fenced-off area called 'the lists'. At a given signal, they would charge. The thundering of hooves was followed by the clash of lance on shield as each knight tried to unhorse his opponent.

A herald proclaimed the names of the participants as they entered the lists and kept a tally of the scores. Points were awarded for breaking a lance on an opponent's shield, for striking his helmet or body armour and – best of all – for unhorsing him.

If a knight was unhorsed in the joust but not badly hurt, the combat could continue with swords on foot. A knight could indicate his wish to end the joust by removing his helmet.

Ladies often gave a token of their favour to a chosen knight to wear in the tournament. He fought in her honour and if he did well, the glory was hers.

The Tourney

Tournaments probably began in the 11th century and were originally mock battles or 'tourneys' where opposing teams of knights and their followers charged at each other across open fields, fighting with lances and swords. It was good practice for battle, but crops were ruined and many died from their wounds or suffocated inside their helmets because of the heat and dust. Gradually, rules were introduced to make tournaments safer. The combat area was made smaller to make judging easier, and blunted lances (or lances fitted with a three-pronged crown or 'coronel' which spread the impact) were introduced to reduce fatalities. The tilt – a barrier separating jousting knights – was introduced in the 15th century to prevent collisions.

A victorious knight could claim the horse and armour of his defeated opponent and ransom money for prisoners captured in the tourney.

Some knights travelled from one tournament to another, amassing a fortune from their winnings.

Feasts

Medieval feasts were lavish occasions. The baron himself would sit at the centre of the 'high' table – a table raised on a platform across one end of the hall. Below him, less important guests, retainers and servants would sit at tressel tables stretching the length of the hall.

When everyone was ready, pages would arrive with jugs of water, basins and napkins so that the feasters could wash their hands, then the first elaborate dishes would be brought in. Often, there would be three separate courses, each one consisting of meat, fish, and numerous sweets and puddings – all served together! Between the courses acrobats, jugglers and minstrels would entertain the guests.

Food was often elaborately decorated. Feathers might be put back on cooked swans or peacocks to make them look life-like. And vegetable dyes were used to colour food, which was sometimes even gilded with gold.

All Together

Only the baron and his guests at high table had individual plates (made from pewter, silver or gold) and personal cups. Everyone else ate from a 'trencher' – a stale piece of bread that soaked up grease and sauces and could be eaten if a guest was really hungry.

On the lower tables food was served in 'messes' or bowls that two or four people ('mess-mates') might share, fishing out pieces of meat with their fingers and putting them on their trenchers. They also shared drinking vessels. Most people ate with their personal knife, often engraved with their initials, a spoon and their fingers. There were no forks. Even so, good manners and courtesy to fellow diners were expected and considered the mark of a good upbringing.

No food was ever wasted. Dogs scavenged under the tables for tasty tit-bits and, at the end of the meal, the trenchers were taken to the castle gates and given to the poor.

A cupbearer stood behind the baron to make sure his cup was always full of wine, and royal guests might bring a 'taster' with them. The taster had to try every dish his master was going to eat. If the food was poisoned the taster would die, not the king or prince!

MYTHS & LEGENDS

Stories of ghosts can sometimes be explained by known events in a castle's history. But not all hauntings involve human figures; some are seen as lights or lighted windows; others involve animals, including a bear returning to torment castle sentries as it was once tormented by bear-baiting.

Many castles have an interesting story to tell. Throughout their long history they may have weathered sieges, taken part in bloody battles, witnessed betrayals, treachery and tragedy and been the site of murders and executions. It is hardly surprising that many are thought to be haunted by uneasy spirits. There are tales of murdered kings, queens and princes reappearing in ghostly form in their former castles or roaming the site of their execution. Some are said to appear without the head they lost on the executioner's block. In other castles people claim you can hear the phantom drumming of an invisible drummer boy. Beds may appear to have been slept in, although the room is locked, and figures glide silently along the battlements before vanishing from sight.

The ghostly forms of a majestic figure leading a procession of mounted warriors have been reported near Cadbury on Midsummer's Eve. Could this be King Arthur and the knights of the Round Table?

The Legend of King Arthur

One of the greatest legends of all is the story of King Arthur and the knights of the Round Table. King Arthur was probably a Celtic warlord of the 6th century who led his people in battle against Anglo-Saxon invaders. But the legend that has been passed on through the years – and was very popular in medieval times – tells of a king with a castle at Camelot and a court of valiant knights who battled against evil, and undertook quests in search of a priceless chalice called the Holy Grail. Although no one can be certain that Arthur existed, many believe he was born at Tintagel Castle in Cornwall, and that the site of Camelot is Cadbury Castle in Somerset, where it is said he has been seen in ghostly processions with his knights.

Not far from Cadbury lies the ancient abbey of Glastonbury. It was here in 1191 that the monks discovered the bodies of a tall man and a woman buried in the fashion of a Celtic prince. A lead cross identified the grave as that of King Arthur.

The Castle Sleeps

Castle life continued in much the same way for several centuries. Improvements continued to be made and by the early 1400s the villeins on the castle estates were given their freedom. Gradually the need for a stronghold diminished. Noble families no longer required the protection of a garrison, nor did they have to supply the king with knights and men-at-arms, since there was now a permanent army.

Many members of the nobility built comfortable new manor houses nearby and castles often fell into disrepair.

Even so, as you wander through the deserted ruins of medieval castles, you can still imagine the music of minstrels, the cries of pages wrestling and sword-fighting, and knights shouting orders in the heat of battle…